THE GREEKS POP-UP

PAM MARA

Text GERALD JENKINS

CONTENTS.

TARQUIN PUBLICATIONS
in association with
BRITISH MUSEUM PUBLICATIONS LTD

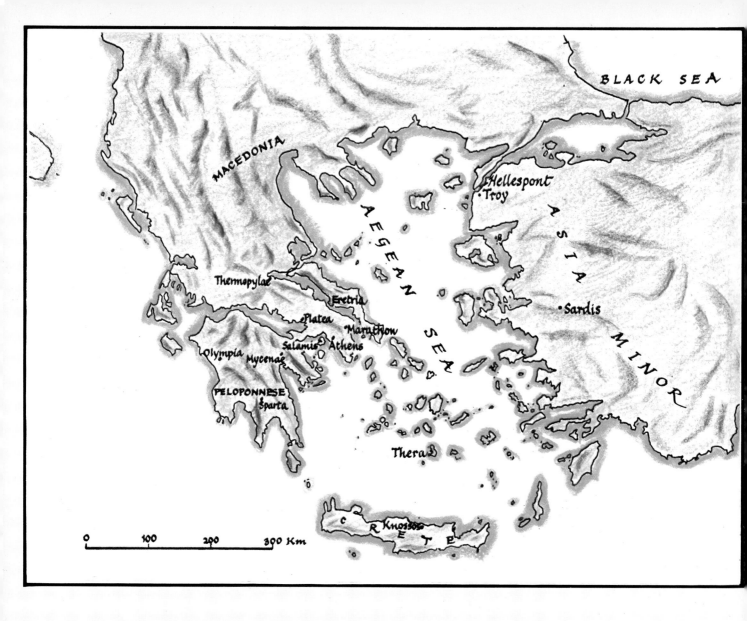

BLACK SEA

MACEDONIA

AEGEAN SEA

Hellespont
Troy

ASIA

Sardis

MINOR

Thermopylae

Eretria

Platea

Marathon

Olympia
Mycenae
Salamis
Athens

PELOPONNESE
Sparta

Thera

0   100   200   300 Km

CRETE
Knossos

©1996:   Pam Mara
©1984:   Previous Edition
I.S.B.N.:   0 906212 33 2
Design: Pam Mara
Printing: Ancient House Press, Ipswich

CE

Tarquin Publications
Stradbroke
Diss
Norfolk IP21 5JP
England

This book was produced in association with British Museum Publications Ltd.

EXCELLENCE IN ALL THINGS

Pericles

For centuries the Greeks have exerted a curious fascination over the minds and imaginations of people all over the world. We wonder today how such a small population, originating from a poor and mountainous country, could possibly have produced so many individuals of outstanding talent and ability in so many different fields. The Greeks did not invent the alphabet or writing, but we are amazed that they should create so many memorable books and tell so many fascinating stories. There are few adults anywhere who did not hear in childhood at least some of the Greek myths and legends and the adventures and misfortunes of their gods and heroes.

In the second century BC, the Roman legions were able to conquer Greece without much difficulty and they undoubtedly knew more than the Greeks about fighting, power and administration. However, the Romans were always unsure of themselves in the face of Greek learning, art and thought. It was commonplace to employ Greek slaves to educate Roman children and to send older sons to University in Athens. Although the Romans built theatres wherever they went, many of the plays performed there were translated from the Greek or were based on Greek stories. When the Roman Empire split in two, the official language of the Eastern Empire was Greek, although they still called themselves Romans. And the Eastern Empire lasted for a thousand years after Rome itself was sacked and the West was overrun.

In modern times, doctors still swear the Hippocratic Oath, first put forward by Hippocrates in about 400 BC. Historians still look back to the "Fathers of History", Thucydides, Herodotus and Xenophon. Mathematicians use the theorems of Pythagoras, Apollonius or Euclid. Modern philosophers still study three of the greatest philosophers there have ever been, Socrates, Plato and Aristotle. Schoolchildren learn "Archimedes's Principle" or see a simple jet engine devised by Hero. Eratosthenes proved that the earth was a sphere and calculated its circumference almost seventeen hundred years before Columbus set sail for America with a crew who believed they would fall off the flat earth. Architects, sculptors and potters everywhere have used Greek originals for inspiration. There are literally thousands of buildings which show a strong Greek influence, from the Bank of England in London, to the Pantheon in Paris and the White House in Washington.

Above all, the Greeks believed in the freedom of the individual under a law passed by a free assembly of the people. Democracy, free speech and free thought are very powerful ideas, but perhaps the most powerful of all is the idea of "excellence in all things". We hope that this book conveys something of their remarkable achievements and draws attention to the fundamental contribution they have made to the development of civilisation.

"Future ages will wonder at us, as the present age wonders at us now"

GENERAL INSTRUCTIONS — How to make your own Pop-Up Book

With this book you can have all the fun of constructing six pop-up scenes and making for yourself an interesting souvenir which tells the story of the Greeks and their place in history.

You will see that some pages of this book are folded in an unusual way to give what are called 'wings', and on them are the pieces you need to make the pop-up scenes. On certain pages there are additional mini pop-ups as well as the main scene and you will find some extra pieces for these on a special page at the back.

TYPE OF GLUE

We particularly recommend a petroleum based glue like UHU or Bostick Clear. Good results can also be obtained with a white latex glue like Copydex. *DO NOT USE* a water based glue or paste which will cause the pages to buckle. If in doubt, do a small trial first.

SCORING

Paper is scored so that it will fold cleanly and pop-up crisply. The best method is to rule along the score lines with a ball-point pen which has run out of ink. Experienced model makers can use a craft knife, but it needs care not to cut right through the paper. Scoring is very important.

HOW TO PREPARE THE BASES

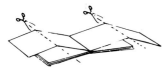

1. Open out the 'wings' and then cut them off along the folds. Cut off all 12 wings.
2. You will see at the back of the book a page of five minicovers. Remove it from the book by cutting along the printed 'cut' line.
3. You now have a book with a single blank page opposite these instructions, a single blank page opposite the instructions at the back and five pairs of facing blank pages.

   The next step is to glue each of the pairs of facing blank pages back to back to double the strength of the bases of the scenes.

4. Spread glue smoothly about 1—1½ cm wide all round the edge on one of each pair. The blue tone on this page shows roughly the extent of glue needed. Gently press the pages together, starting at the spine and smooth outwards from the centre.

5. When all five pairs are done, the bases of scenes 2, 3, 4, 5, are ready and you can make up these scenes. See the instructions below.

6. When scenes 2, 3, 4, 5 are complete and these instructions are no longer needed, spread glue on the blue tone on this page and then glue it to the blank page opposite. Then you can make Scene 1.

7. When you have made up all the mini pop-ups and do not need those instructions any more, glue the blank back page similarly. Then complete Scene 6.

HOW TO ASSEMBLE EACH SCENE

The recommended order is to make scene 4 first, then 5, 2, 3, 1 and finally Scene 6.

For each Scene

1. Cut out each piece from the two wings keeping well away from the outline.
2. Score along all fold lines, dotted and solid.
3. Fold away from you to give a hill fold and towards you to give a valley fold. Crease firmly.
4. Cut out precisely.
5. For each scene there is a plan diagram which shows the position of the pieces. Start with piece 1 and work in order.
6. Each letter on a flap corresponds to a letter on the base or to a letter on another piece. Glue them in alphabetical order A, B, C.
7. Flaps marked 'glue behind', do not have a corresponding letter printed behind, but where there is any possibility of such a flap being glued in the wrong position, there are black lines on the base to help with alignment.

VALLEY FOLD

HILL FOLD

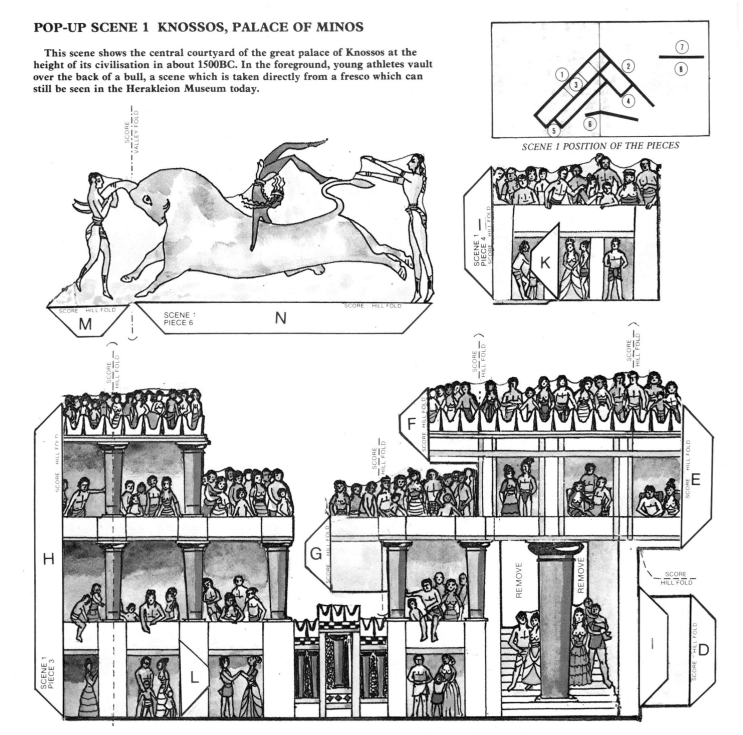

POP-UP SCENE 1 KNOSSOS, PALACE OF MINOS

This scene shows the central courtyard of the great palace of Knossos at the height of its civilisation in about 1500BC. In the foreground, young athletes vault over the back of a bull, a scene which is taken directly from a fresco which can still be seen in the Herakleion Museum today.

SCENE 1 POSITION OF THE PIECES

SCORE VALLEY FOLD

SCORE HILL FOLD

M

SCENE 1 PIECE 6

N

SCORE HILL FOLD

SCENE 1 PIECE 4

SCORE HILL FOLD

K

SCORE HILL FOLD

F

SCORE HILL FOLD

E

H

SCORE HILL FOLD

G

SCORE HILL FOLD

SCENE 1 PIECE 3

L

REMOVE

REMOVE

SCORE HILL FOLD

I

D

SCORE HILL FOLD

THE MINOANS

There is a land called Crete in the midst of the wine dark sea, a fair land and a rich, begirt with water, and there are many men innumerable and ninety cities... And among these cities is the mighty Knossos, wherein Minos when he was nine years old began to rule...

So said Homer in about 700 BC. Most people thought that this was just a story or legend, but a few people believed that a great city would be found at Knossos, just as others had already been found at Troy and Mycenae. After the end of the Turkish occupation of Crete in 1900, Sir Arthur Evans started to excavate the mound at Knossos. Almost immediately he discovered the remains of a great palace and evidence of an advanced civilisation quite different from any on the mainland. He called the people 'The Minoans' after the legendary King Minos and then devoted the rest of his life to excavating and restoring the Palace.

Other palaces were found across the island and gradually an understanding of these previously unknown people was built up. The Minoans seemed to have been a peace-loving people. No weapons of war were found and their palaces were not fortified. They decorated their rooms with lively frescoes of dolphins, monkeys, flowers and animals. They wore colourful clothes and had elaborate hairstyles and much jewellery. Countless workrooms and stores show just how rich the Kingdom of Crete was at the height of its power.

From time to time earthquakes shook down the palaces, but they were always rebuilt on a grander scale until in about 1450 BC there was a greater disaster and the Minoan civilisation received a blow from which it was never to recover. It is not certain exactly what happened but perhaps it was connected with the massive volcanic eruption on the island of Thera, 100 km to the North. It is also not certain whether the Greeks from the mainland occupied Crete before this final disaster or shortly afterwards, but we do know they came. A legend hints at it and their writing proved it.

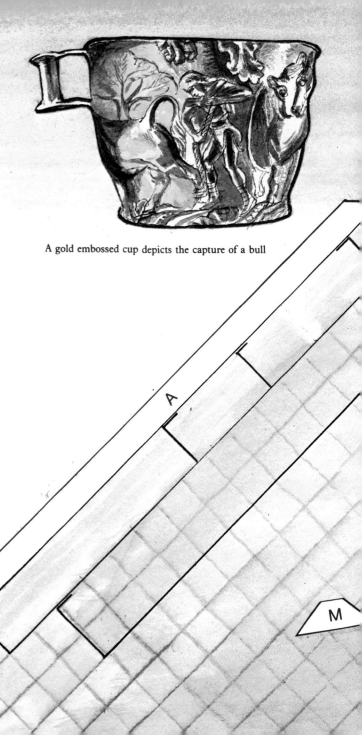

A gold embossed cup depicts the capture of a bull

THESEUS AND THE MINOTAUR

The legend says that King Minos demanded from Athens every year a tribute of seven youths and seven maidens. These young people were fed to the minotaur, a beast which was part man, part bull and which lived in a labyrinth beneath the palace of Knossos. Theseus, whose father was king of Athens, took the place of one of the youths and set off in the black-sailed ship to Crete. On arriving there he insisted on being the first to be sacrificed to the Minotaur and charmed Ariadne, the daughter of King Minos into helping him. She gave him a sword and a ball of thread. Thus Theseus was able to slay the Minotaur and then find his way back out of the maze by following the scarlet thread. He took Ariadne as far as Naxos and then abandoned her and returned in triumph as he hoped to Athens. Unfortunately he forgot to change the black sails for white ones and so his father King Aegeus thought that this meant Theseus had been killed. In his grief, Aegeus jumped into the sea and perished and that is why that sea is known as the Aegean.

WHO WERE THE MINOANS?

In the palace of Knossos and later at other sites on the mainland archaeologists found thousands of clay tablets covered with writing. They were in two styles, the older called 'Linear A' and the later one called 'Linear B'. After many years of work, a young English architect called Michael Ventris and Professor Chadwick managed to show that 'Linear B' was in fact Greek. Everyone was astonished, as it was by far the oldest known use of Greek. The tablets proved to be simply lists and palace records, but were fascinating none the less. So far, 'Linear A' has not been deciphered, as there is much less of it to work on. However it looks as if it is the ancient language of the original Minoans. It seems that once the island was conquered by the Greeks, Linear A was not a convenient script for writing Greek and so it was adapted into Linear B. This is one of the reasons why we know that the Greeks came to Crete. Perhaps the legend of Theseus and the Minotaur grew out of the story of the Greeks from Athens finally overcoming the power of the Minoans.

The dolphin fresco from the Queen's room at Knossos

This scene shows the famous throne room at the palace of Knossos. The plastered walls are covered with colourful paintings which are called frescoes. From these frescoes and others elsewhere in the palace we can get a tantalising glimpse of the elegant and sophisticated civilisation which existed in Crete about 3,500 years ago.

KNOSSOS – PALACE OF MINOS

This scene shows the main courtyard of the great palace at Knossos on the island of Crete. The highly developed Minoan civilisation dominated the Aegean until the Minoans were finally taken over by the Greeks from the mainland. In the Arena, young athletes are leaping over the back of a bull. It is not known how this was done or why, but this picture is taken from an original fresco which can still be seen in Herakleion Museum today.

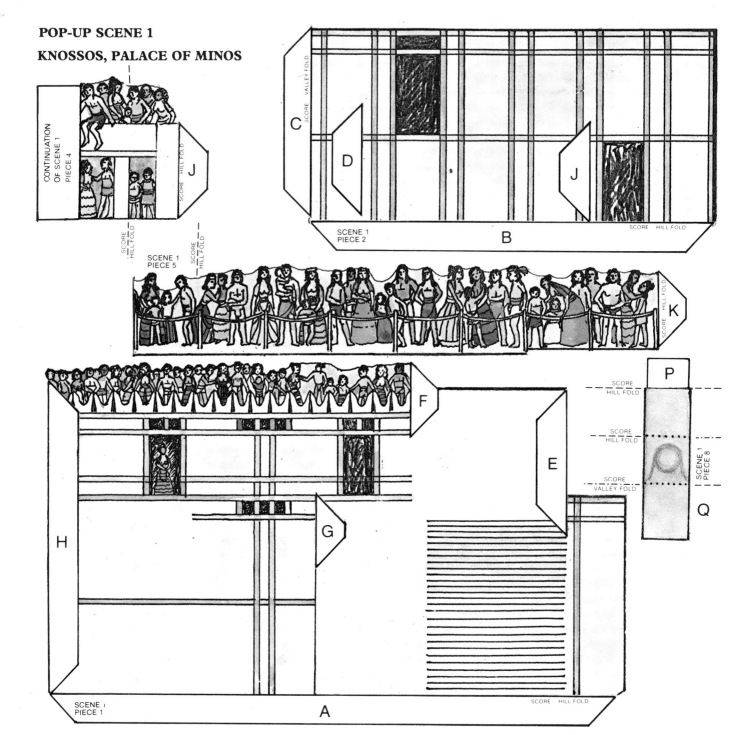

POP-UP SCENE 1
KNOSSOS, PALACE OF MINOS

CONTINUATION OF SCENE 1 PIECE 4

SCORE HILL FOLD — J

SCORE HILL FOLD

SCORE HILL FOLD

SCENE 1 PIECE 5

SCORE VALLEY FOLD — C

D

J

SCENE 1 PIECE 2

B

SCORE HILL FOLD

SCORE HILL FOLD — K

F

E

G

H

SCORE HILL FOLD — P

SCORE HILL FOLD

SCORE VALLEY FOLD

SCENE 1 PIECE 8

Q

SCENE 1 PIECE 1

A

SCORE HILL FOLD

POP-UP SCENE 2 THE LION GATE AT MYCENAE

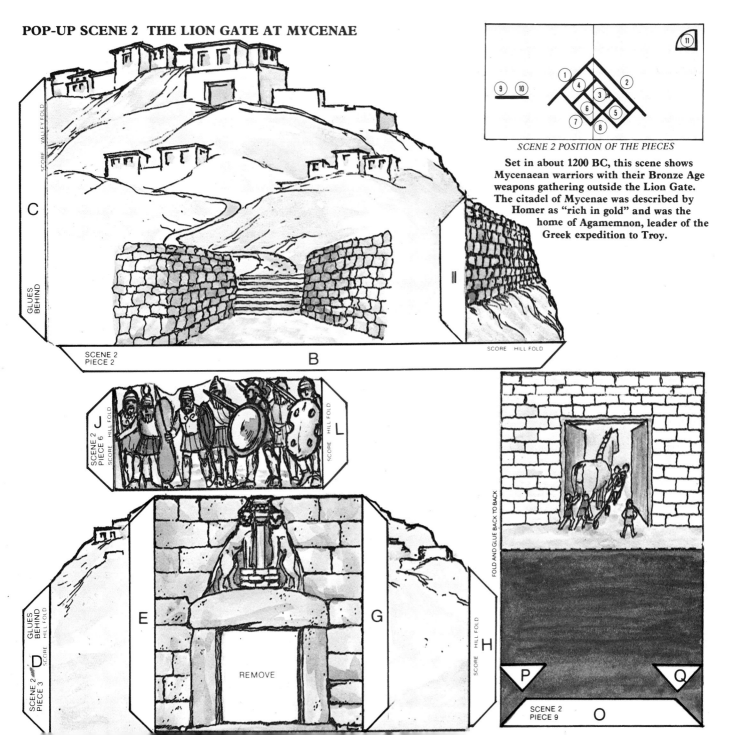

SCENE 2 POSITION OF THE PIECES

Set in about 1200 BC, this scene shows Mycenaean warriors with their Bronze Age weapons gathering outside the Lion Gate. The citadel of Mycenae was described by Homer as "rich in gold" and was the home of Agamemnon, leader of the Greek expedition to Troy.

C

SCORE VALLEY FOLD

GLUES BEHIND

SCENE 2 PIECE 2

B

SCORE HILL FOLD

J

SCENE 2 PIECE 6

SCORE HILL FOLD

L

SCORE HILL FOLD

D

SCENE 2 PIECE 3

GLUES BEHIND

SCORE HILL FOLD

E

G

H

SCORE HILL FOLD

REMOVE

FOLD AND GLUE BACK TO BACK

P

Q

SCENE 2 PIECE 9

O

HOMER AND THE TROJAN WAR

The Iliad and The Odyssey are two great epic poems composed about 2700 years ago, but still vivid and exciting to read today. Not much is known about Homer himself, but in ancient times his poems were recited at feasts and festivals long before reading and writing became widespread. They do not tell the whole story of the Trojan war, which his audience was expected to know about anyway, but concentrated on certain aspects of it with such skill and mastery that they rank among some of the greatest stories ever written in any language.

Troy was a city in Asia Minor and Paris was one of its princes. Paris fell in love with Helen, the wife of King Menelaus of Sparta and persuaded her to leave her husband and come back with him to Troy. Menelaus was furious, and so was his brother King Agamemnon of Mycenae. They gathered together a great army and set sail for Troy, ready to teach the Trojans a lesson. They landed close to Troy, but the city had strong walls and successfully resisted for nine long years. It is only at this point that the story of the Iliad begins. Incidentally another name for Troy was Ilium and that explains the name of the poem.

The Greeks had a great fighter or hero called Achilles, but he quarrelled with Agamemnon over a slave girl and refused to fight. On the Trojan side the best fighter was Hector and he proposed that since the war had gone on for so long it should be settled by a duel between Paris and Menelaus alone. They fought and Menelaus won, or rather he nearly did. Throughout the battle the gods had interfered on both sides and in this case the goddess Aphrodite spirited Paris away and saved him. The general fighting broke out' again and with Achilles sulking in his tent the Greeks were soon in difficulty. The Trojans drove them back to their ships and even managed to set fire to one of them. Even then, Achilles would not help, but he did lend his famous armour to his friend Patroclus. The day was saved but Patroclus was killed. Achilles was seized with a great fury, fought Hector, killed him and then dragged his body three times around the walls of Troy behind his chariot. The Iliad ends with the funeral of Hector, but still the war continued.

Achilles was killed by an arrow in the heel fired by Paris but guided to its target by the god Apollo. Paris himself was killed, but still the war did not come to an end.

The city of Troy was totally destroyed and at last the Greeks were free to return home. The journey would normally take two or three weeks, but due to bad weather and the action of the gods it took Odysseus ten years! The Odyssey tells the story of the adventures and misfortunes which delayed his return to Ithaca, and of the experiences of his wife Penelope and son Telemachus. There is not space here to tell of his adventures and the slaughter of the suitors in the great hall, but it is a tale worth reading, and one which has fascinated children and adults for approaching three thousand years.

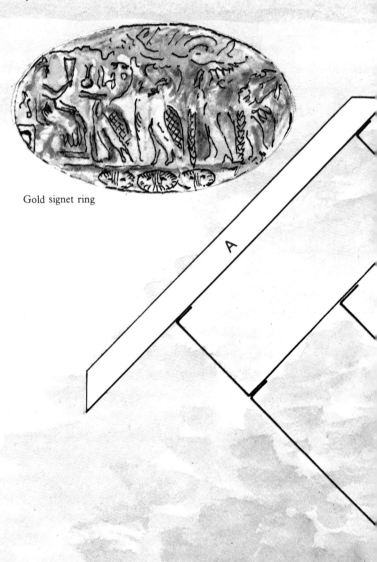

Gold signet ring

R

Then the crafty Odysseus had a huge wooden horse made, inside which some Greek soldiers could hide. The rest of the Greeks sailed away as if they had finally given up, leaving the wooden horse in front of the city. The Trojans thought the war was over and in spite of warnings "not to trust the Greeks even when they are bearing gifts", they dragged the wooden horse inside the city. That night the Greeks broke out and opened up the gates to let in the main army which had secretly sailed back again.

AGAMEMNON OF MYCENAE, FACT OR FICTION?

During the 19th century most scholars regarded the vivid world described in The Iliad and The Odyssey as purely a work of fiction. Others, including a wealthy German merchant called Heinrich Schliemann believed that the stories were based on real events and real places. He set out to prove it by excavating at Troy and then turned his attention to Mycenae. In a whirlwind season of eleven weeks he excavated a circle of graves just inside the Lion Gate and found a remarkable treasure. There were six deep graves, each containing from 2 to 5 skeletons and a great collection of objects in bronze, silver, ivory and above all gold. Mycenae was indeed "rich in gold" just as Homer had said. And perhaps most exciting of all to Schliemann there was a golden death mask of a dignified warrior.

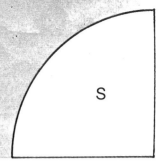

Schliemann sent a triumphant telegram to the King of the Hellenes.

However, further work and investigation proved that he was mistaken and that the occupants of the graves had probably lived about 300 years before Agamemnon and the Trojan War. It did not diminish the wonder of the find which can still be seen today in the National Museum in Athens. Further excavation in other parts of Greece and elsewhere showed that Mycenae was just one centre of an extensive civilisation which we now know as "Mycenaean". We know they spoke Greek, but the Ancient Greeks and Homer called their Bronze Age ancestors "The Achaeans", "The Danaans" or "The Argives". At first the Mycenaeans were influenced by the Minoans on Crete, but later they developed their own culture and even conquered Crete itself.

At first the Mycenaean palaces were lightly fortified but later they were surrounded by huge walls called "cyclopean" by the later Greeks because it seemed they must have been built by Giants. At Mycenae itself the Lion Gate was built and the walls extended in about 1300 BC, a hundred years before the probable date of the Trojan war. Probably Agamemnon did stride through the Lion Gate, but the death mask we call "The mask of Agamemnon" was already buried under the ground a few metres away, and had been for a full 200 years.

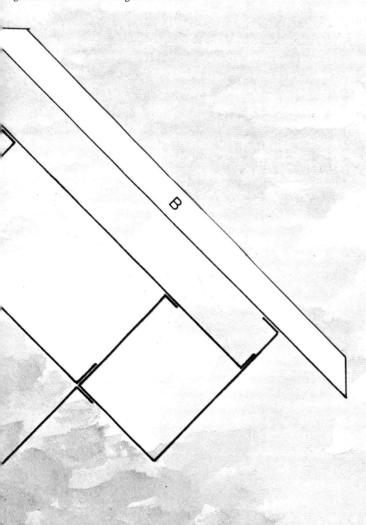

THE LION GATE AT MYCENAE

The Lion Gate and the huge walls which surround the ancient citadel of Mycenae still stand today. In this scene, set after the end of the Trojan War, some Mycenaean soldiers with their bronze weapons gather outside the Gate, ready to repel the Dorian invaders. This invasion was probably not a swift military campaign, but more an infiltration of a whole people. The Dorians were also Greeks, but were far less civilised at the time than the Mycenaeans. However they had iron weapons and in the end were victorious, bringing in a dark age which was to last for more than three hundred years. Throughout this period memories of the glorious past were carried down by word of mouth only. Then the alphabet was invented and the stories and legends which we can read today were written down.

POP-UP SCENE 2 THE LION GATE AT MYCENAE

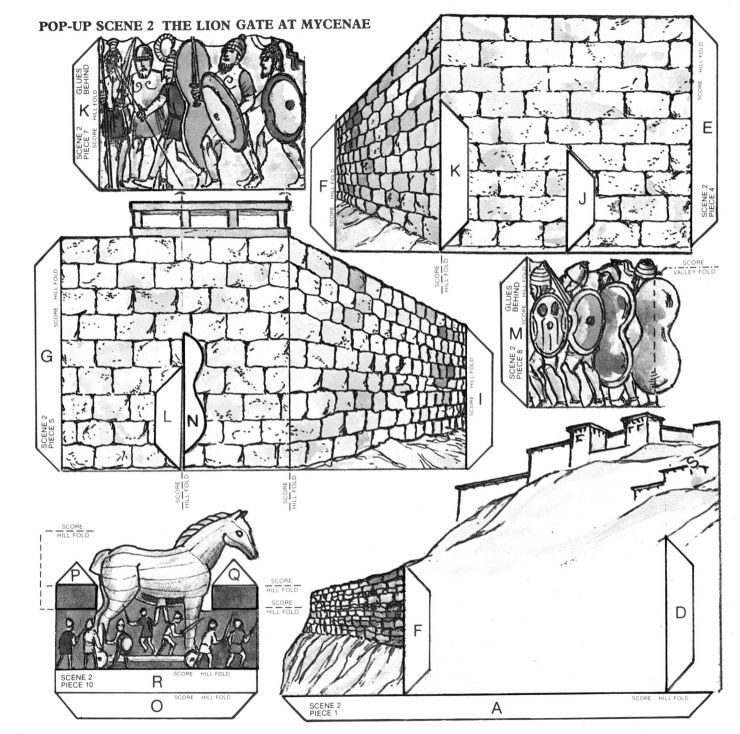

GLUES BEHIND

K

SCENE 2 PIECE 7

HILL FOLD SCORE

F SCORE HILL FOLD

K

J

SCORE HILL FOLD

E

SCENE 2 PIECE 4

SCORE HILL FOLD

SCORE VALLEY FOLD

GLUES BEHIND

M

SCENE 2 PIECE 8

SCORE HILL FOLD

G

SCENE 2 PIECE 5

SCORE HILL FOLD

L N

I

SCORE HILL FOLD

SCORE HILL FOLD

SCORE HILL FOLD

SCORE HILL FOLD

P Q

SCORE HILL FOLD

SCORE HILL FOLD

SCENE 2 PIECE 10

R

SCORE HILL FOLD

O

SCORE HILL FOLD

S

F

D

SCENE 2 PIECE 1

A

SCORE HILL FOLD

POP-UP SCENE 3
THE BATTLE OF SALAMIS

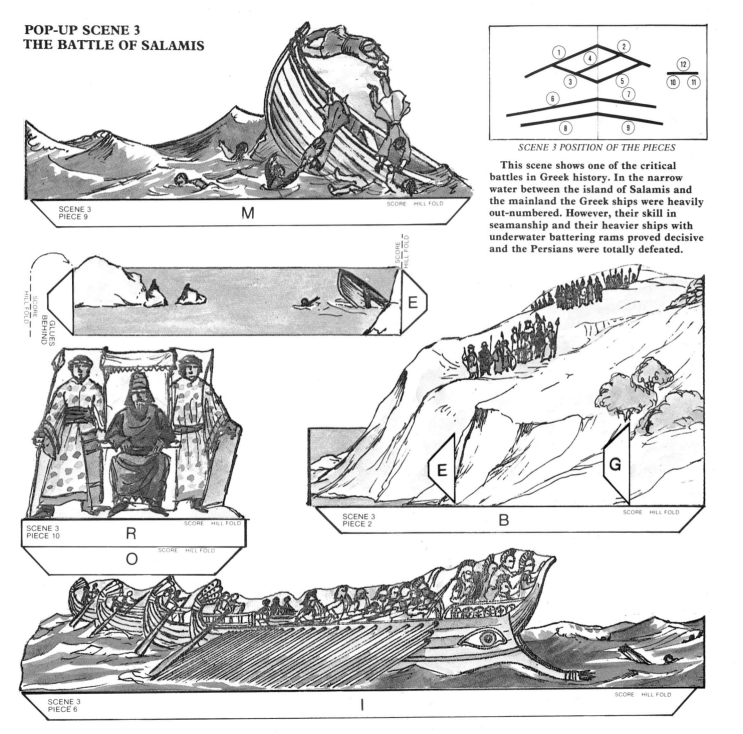

SCENE 3
PIECE 9

M

SCORE   HILL FOLD

SCENE 3 POSITION OF THE PIECES

This scene shows one of the critical battles in Greek history. In the narrow water between the island of Salamis and the mainland the Greek ships were heavily out-numbered. However, their skill in seamanship and their heavier ships with underwater battering rams proved decisive and the Persians were totally defeated.

SCORE
HILL FOLD

E

SCORE
HILL FOLD

GLUES
BEHIND

SCENE 3
PIECE 10

R

SCORE   HILL FOLD

O

SCORE   HILL FOLD

E

G

SCENE 3
PIECE 2

B

SCORE   HILL FOLD

SCENE 3
PIECE 6

I

SCORE   HILL FOLD

THE WAR WITH PERSIA

Most of Greece is rocky and mountainous and there was never enough good valley land to feed a growing population. So, from earliest times, bands of Greeks set sail in their ships to trade with neighbouring countries and to look for fertile land where they might settle. At first these new colonies were founded close to the Greek mainland, but gradually they settled at suitable places further and further along the coasts of Asia Minor and the Black Sea. There were sometimes conflicts with the native people of the areas, but mostly the payment of taxes to the local chieftain or king was sufficient to make them welcome. The situation changed later when the Persians conquered all of Asia Minor and tried to demand much higher payments. The Greek cities were outraged at this and there was a series of revolts, helped and supported by the mainland cities of Athens and Eretria. Although in the end the Persians crushed the revolts, it was only after the city of Sardis was burned to the ground. The Persian King Darius was furious and swore that he would teach the mainland Greeks a lesson as well. He ordered a slave to remind him three times a day about the Greeks so that he would keep his hatred alive while the preparations for an invasion were made.

THE BATTLE OF MARATHON

The Persians first invaded Eretria and the Athenians prepared to fight. They sent Pheidippides to run to Sparta to ask for help but the Spartans said that they couldn't fight until after the next full moon. So the Athenians, with the help of some Plateans set off to Marathon where the Persians were camped on some level ground near the sea. Although the Greeks were out-numbered two to one, they charged down the hill and drove the Persians into

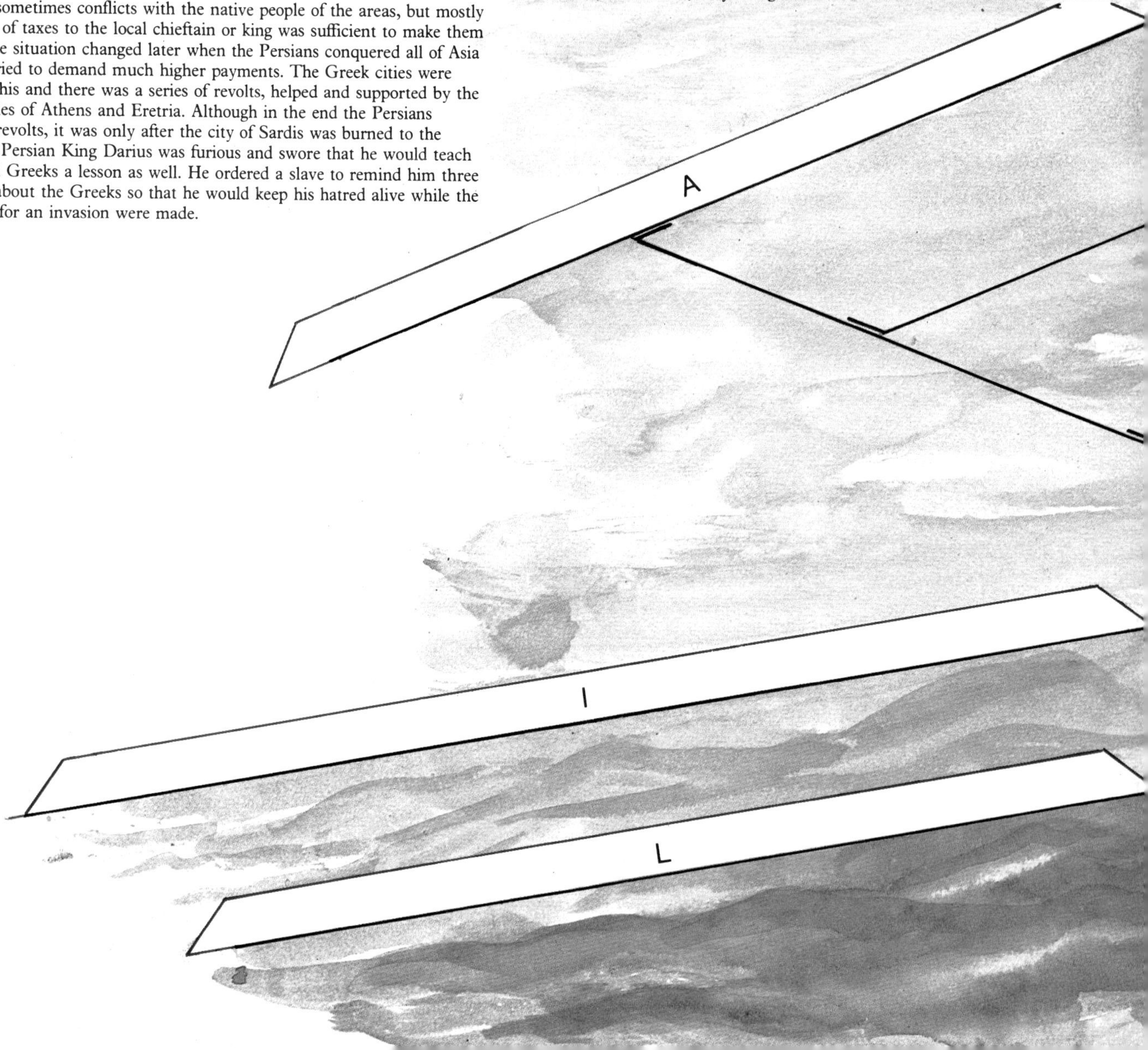

A

I

L

a marsh, totally defeating them. Pheidippides fought in the battle and then ran to Athens, a distance of 24 miles, with news of the victory. However, the effort was too much for him and he was just able to gasp "Rejoice, we conquer", before he collapsed and died.

In the battle the Persians had lost 6000 men and the Greeks only 192, but the Persian fleet was still intact and it sailed to Athens. However, the Athenians marched back at full speed and waited to repel any further attacks. When the Persians saw the troops on the shore they gave up and sailed away.

So ended the first Persian invasion.

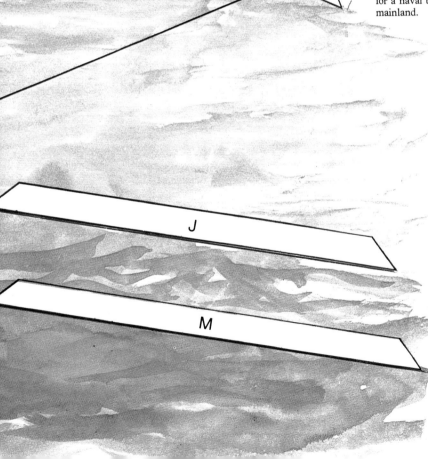

THE SECOND INVASION

Ten years later, the new Persian King Xerxes decided that he would conquer Greece with a huge army marching overland. To cross over between Asia and Europe he built a bridge of boats across the Hellespont and his army was able to march across. It was said that the Persian army was 200,000 strong and they drank the rivers dry as they crossed over them. As the army marched along the coast, the enormous Persian fleet sailed with it, a terrifying prospect for the Greeks. This time the Spartans did fight – and most bravely. At a narrow pass called Thermopylae, a band of 300 Spartans under their King Leonidas held up the entire Persian army for two days before being surrounded. Not one Spartan survived.

Athens was evacuated as the Persians moved South, except for a few townspeople who tried to hold the Acropolis. However they were soon overpowered and killed and then the city was set on fire. Things looked very black indeed for the Greeks who had gathered on the island of Salamis. The oracle at Delphi, which was always hard to understand had said that the Athenians should "trust their wooden walls". Since their city was now on fire, the Athenian General Themistocles convinced everyone that it really meant their wooden ships. The Athenians still had 200 ships and so they prepared for a naval battle to be fought in the narrow waters between Salamis and the mainland.

Against the Greek fleet of 200 ships Xerxes had 1000 and he was so sure that his fleet would win that he set up a throne on the slopes of mount Aegalos to watch.

However, the heavier Greek ships with their high sides or wooden walls and their underwater battering rams proved too much for the Persians. In the constricted waters of the bay, the superior skill and tactics of the Greeks was enough to win a most decisive victory. They were even able to kill Xerxes's brother.

THE BATTLE OF SALAMIS

With Athens already lost and their ships heavily outnumbered, the Greeks fought a desperate battle against the Persian fleet and won an outstanding victory.

Shocked by their defeat, the Persians withdrew their army to the North for the winter ready to fight again in the spring. However, when spring came the Greeks won another great victory at Platea, this time on land. After this, the Persian army withdrew in some confusion and the threat of invasion and occupation was finally ended.

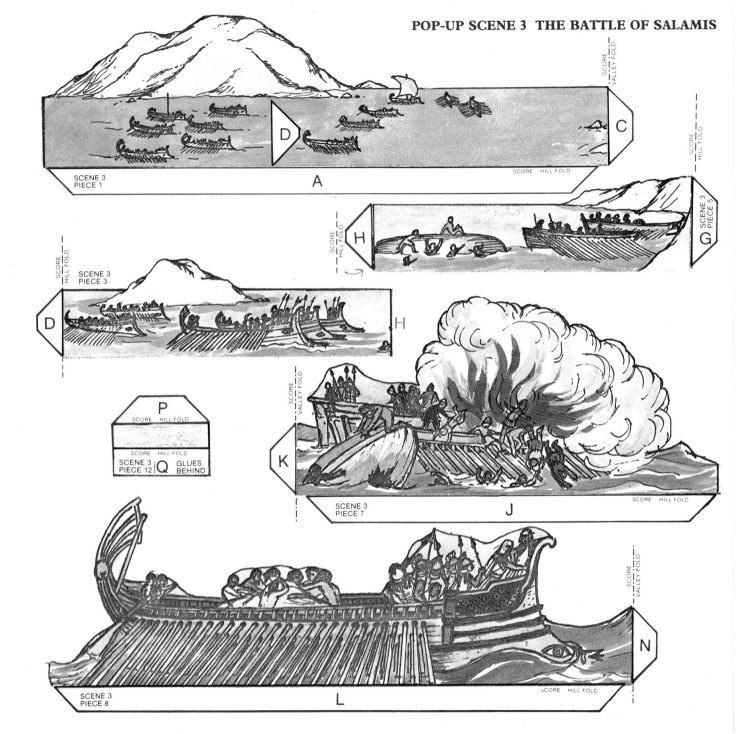

POP-UP SCENE 3 THE BATTLE OF SALAMIS

POP-UP SCENE 4 THE GOLDEN AGE OF ATHENS

SCENE 4 POSITION OF THE PIECES

In this scene, citizens and philosophers meet in the Market Place to discuss the latest news. Behind, and dominating the sky line of Athens then as it does today is the Acropolis or "city on high".

SCORE VALLEY FOLD
GLUES BEHIND
K
SCORE HILL FOLD

SCENE 4 PIECE 6
I

L →

REMOVE   REMOVE   REMOVE

SCENE 4 PIECE 8

M →

SCENE 4 PIECE 2
B
SCORE HILL FOLD

SCENE 4 PIECE 1
A

SCORE VALLEY FOLD
GLUES BEHIND
C
SCORE HILL FOLD

PHILOSOPHERS

The Greeks had a very high regard for the people who tried to find out the truth about the meaning of life and to understand why people behaved as they did. They called such a person "a philosopher" which means "lover of wisdom".

SOCRATES

Socrates was a great philosopher, but he would not write anything down or give public lectures. He used to stroll about the city, especially the Agora, or Market Place, and talk to anyone who was interested. He particularly liked to talk to self-confident people who considered themselves expert in a certain subject. Then he would ask searching questions trying to find out the truth so that often that person came to realize that he didn't know much after all. This method of arriving at the truth by asking questions is still called "The Socratic Method". Amongst other things he also had a disbelieving and questioning attitude towards the gods. His outspoken ways and irreverent approach to life made him many enemies in high places. He was accused of being a bad influence on the young, was tried and sentenced to be exiled or to be put to death. He chose to die and calmly drank a cup of hemlock, surrounded by his friends.

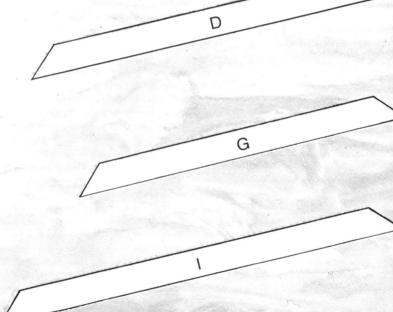

THE PORCH OF THE CARYATIDS

This porch is part of the Erechtheum and still stands today on the north side of the Acropolis. The Erechtheum is a temple with a rather unusual plan because it was built to include several older shrines and was the site of the Mycenaean palace of Athens. According to legend it was the only Mycenaean palace not to fall to the Dorians.

The Athenians regarded themselves as the descendants of the Achaeans and as Ionians, whereas the Spartans were Dorian by descent. Those differences were emphasised during the long war between Athens and Sparta, called 'The Peloponnesian War' and which lasted from 431 to 404 BC and ended with the defeat of Athens.

PLATO

The reason why we know so much about Socrates and the manner in which he met his death is that he had a gifted pupil called Plato who wrote down many of his conversations in what are called "The Dialogues". After the death of Socrates he travelled widely, spoke to many wise men and then founded his own school of philosophy in Athens called "The Academy". It was from Plato that we heard about Atlantis, an island with a marvellous civilisation which sank beneath the sea in a great disaster. Many people have looked for the island, but no-one has found it. Some thought it was in the Atlantic, others that it was in the Aegean and was destroyed when Thera erupted. However, Plato was very interested in how states should be governed and how rulers should behave and so it seems more likely that he invented it in order to put forward his own views of an ideal society.

ARISTOTLE

Aristotle was a pupil of Plato, but his interests were very different. Whereas Plato was interested in what society should be like, Aristotle studied nature and the world as it was. He wrote a history of animals which is still highly regarded. He examined the structure of living things and worked out a classification system for all plants and animals. He studied the weather, human and animal behaviour, society, physics and metaphysics. In a most prolific life he set out the rules and ideas of the scientific method and logic which are the foundation of modern science. For several years he was tutor to Alexander the Great and then returned to Athens to set up his own school of philosophy. He and his pupils used to walk back and forth while discussing their weighty ideas and so they became known as "The Peripatetics", from the Greek "to walk about".

DEMOCRACY

One of the greatest contributions that the Greeks and Athens in particular have given to the world is the idea of democracy. The word itself is Greek. It means "government by the people". The ideal was that every citizen had a say in the assembly and it was the assembly which passed laws, took decisions and appointed the generals and leaders. Once a law was passed by the assembly, then every citizen had to obey it.

THE GOLDEN AGE OF ATHENS

Under Pericles, who was elected leader at the end of the Persian War, Athens flourished. In an impressive show of self-confidence, they set out to rebuild the city and to make it the centre of the civilized world. Never before or since were so many people of exceptional talent or genius gathered together in one place.

In the foreground, some of the outstanding citizens meet in the Agora or market place. Behind, stands the Acropolis and on it the great temple of the Parthenon, built at the time and dedicated to Athene, goddess of wisdom.

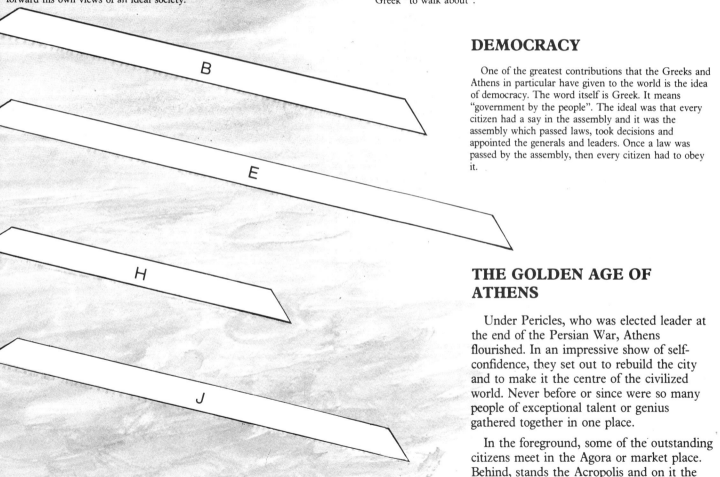

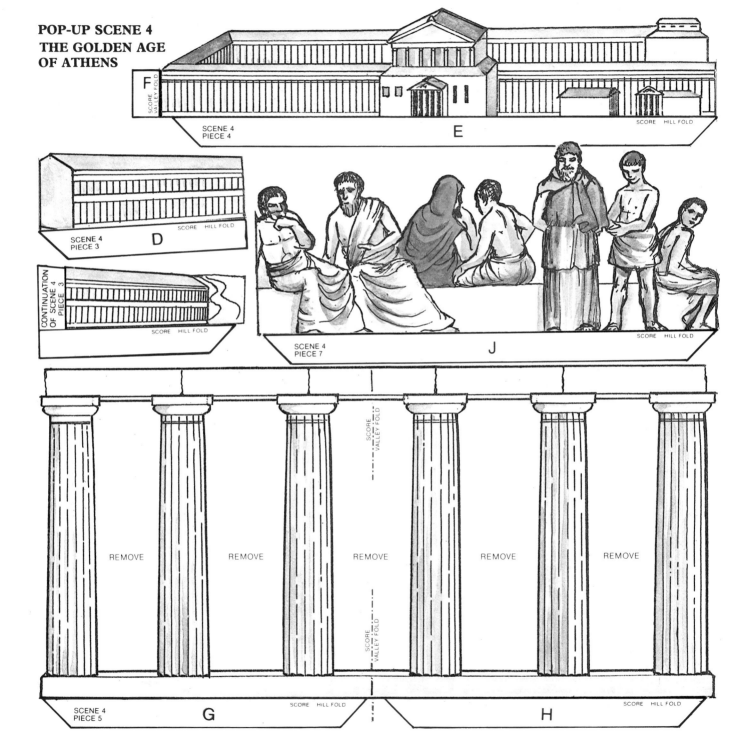

POP-UP SCENE 4
THE GOLDEN AGE
OF ATHENS

F SCORE VALLEY FOLD

SCENE 4
PIECE 4

SCORE HILL FOLD

E

SCENE 4
PIECE 3

SCORE HILL FOLD

D

CONTINUATION OF SCENE 4 PIECE 3

SCORE HILL FOLD

SCENE 4
PIECE 7

SCORE HILL FOLD

J

SCORE VALLEY FOLD

SCORE VALLEY FOLD

REMOVE   REMOVE   REMOVE   REMOVE   REMOVE

SCENE 4
PIECE 5

G

SCORE HILL FOLD

H

SCORE HILL FOLD

POP-UP SCENE 5   THE THEATRE

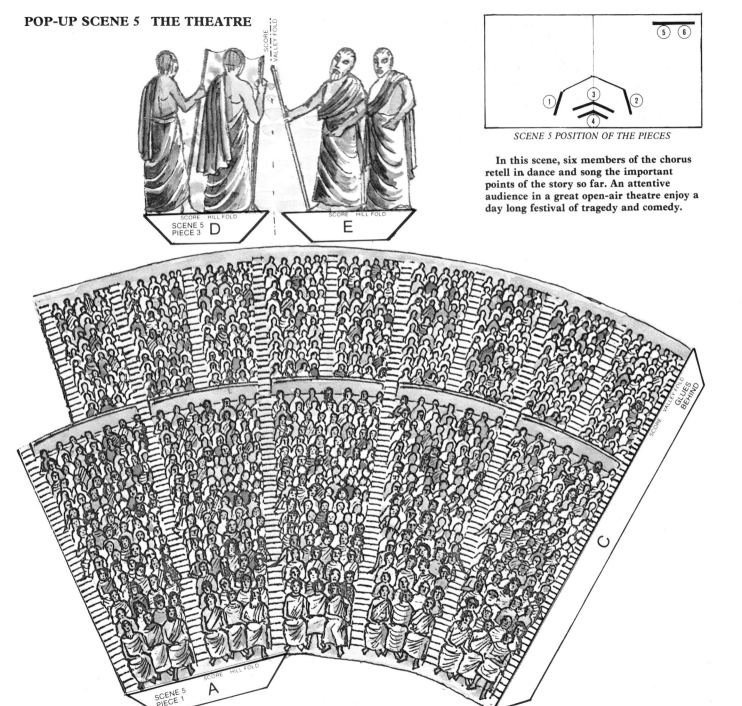

SCORE VALLEY FOLD

SCORE   HILL FOLD
SCENE 5
PIECE 3   **D**

E

SCENE 5 POSITION OF THE PIECES

In this scene, six members of the chorus retell in dance and song the important points of the story so far. An attentive audience in a great open-air theatre enjoy a day long festival of tragedy and comedy.

SCORE VALLEY FOLD
GLUES BEHIND

C

SCORE   HILL FOLD
SCENE 5
PIECE 1   **A**

THE MODERN OLYMPIC GAMES

One of the people fired by the ideals of those ancient Games was a Frenchman, Baron de Coubertin. He proposed that a new series of Olympic Games should be set up, also to be held once every four years. Only amateurs should be able to take part and it would be an opportunity for young people of every nationality to meet and compete in friendly rivalry. The first of the new Olympic Games was held in Athens in 1896 and they have been held ever since except for the War years of 1918, 1940 and 1944. We haven't yet been able to stop wars while the Games are held! In the modern Games there are many more events, including team games. There are also events for women, an idea that the Greeks themselves would have found very peculiar.

THE OLYMPIC FLAME

The symbol of the modern games is the Olympic flame, which burns throughout the meeting. At the opening ceremony, it is lit by a runner with a flaming torch. That flame was first kindled by the rays of the sun at Olympia and then carried by a chain of runners to the stadium, of course making use of planes and ships for parts of the journey where that is necessary.

THE MARATHON

At the first of the modern Olympics, a race of about 24 miles from Marathon to Athens was held in honour of that famous run by Pheidippides. To the great delight of the crowd it was won by a Greek, Loues. Ever since then it has been called "The Marathon", but curiously the modern distance of 26 miles 385 yards was not run in Athens, but from Windsor to London in 1908. It became the official distance for the Olympic Games wherever they are held, in 1924.

THE GAMES

Exercising the body as well as the mind was an important part of Greek life and education. Boys spent several hours each day in training, and while general fitness was obviously very helpful for military skills, it was also admired for its own sake. After the exercise, pupils would wash, anoint themselves with olive oil and then continue with their lessons. Greek statues show clearly the regard for an athletic and well-trained body. This respect for athletic skills was emphasised in festivals of games, sometimes for just one city, but also for all Greeks no matter where they might live. The best known of the "Panhellenic" Games, (the word itself means "all Greeks") were those held at Olympia in the Peloponnese.

The Olympic Games started in 776 BC and were held every four years. They took the form of a festival to the gods and became so important that even wars were interrupted while they were being held. The Games lasted for three days and began with chariot and horse races. Then followed the most important event, the Pentathlon (*Penta* means five, *athlon* means contest). The events were – a long jump, a foot race, javelin, discus and wrestling. At first valuable prizes were given, but later the only prize was a wreath of laurel or wild olive cut from a sacred tree with a golden sickle. Athletes had to swear an oath before taking part that they would not cheat and that they had trained hard for ten months. The final event of the Games was called the Pancration, which means roughly that everything was allowed. It was a form of no-holds-barred wrestling where only biting and eye gouging were forbidden. Since strangling and jumping on an opponent were permissible it is not surprising that sometimes contestants were badly injured or killed.

The Olympic Games continued until they were abolished by the Roman Emperor in AD 393. The ancient stadium at Olympia can still be visited, but it was badly damaged in an earthquake and little remains today. However it is still possible to enter the arena through the ancient archway and then to stand on the starting line and imagine the cheers and excitement of those contests so many years ago.

DRAMA

The Greeks had a great love of drama and can be said to have invented the idea of the theatre as public entertainment. At first, theatres were simply patches of beaten ground with the audience seated nearby on grassy slopes, but gradually splendid theatres seating up to 15,000 people were built in stone and marble. They were usually built into a hillside and the audience often had a spectacular view across the countryside. Many of these theatres have survived and today it is possible to sit in the same seats as the ancient Greeks did all those years ago. At Epidaurus, the ancient theatre is still used for the performance of plays and it is remarkable how well sound carries to the seats right at the back. Every remark and whispered aside can be heard. The theatres were so large that the audience would have had difficulty in seeing the expressions on the faces of the actors, and we must remember that spectacles and binoculars had not been invented. All actors wore large masks which showed the features very boldly. Sometimes a mask had a cheerful expression on one side and a sad one on the other, so that they could change the mood quickly when they had to.

Actors were always men and they used their own voices even when playing the part of women. There were normally only two or three actors on stage at a time, but there was also a chorus of 15 or more who danced, sang and recited to the accompaniment of a pipe. The chorus, again always men, marked the division between the acts and also drew attention to important points in the unfolding of the play.

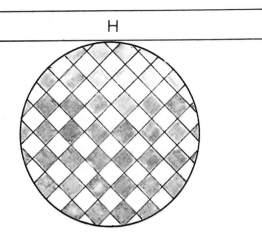

Plays were presented as part of a festival to the god Dionysus and took the form of a competition. When the Ancient Greeks went to the theatre they went for the whole day and saw four different plays, three tragedies and a comedy, with the comedy always coming last. Tragedies were usually based on the stories and legends of the past, although they did not have to be. There were three famous playwrights who wrote tragedies called Aeschylus, Sophocles and Euripides. They wrote many, many plays but only 31 have survived for us to read or act. Even so, they are considered some of the greatest dramatists there have ever been. The comedies were very funny and poked fun at well-known politicians and public figures. The best known of the comedy writers was Aristophanes. Writers had a considerable amount of freedom and even during the Peloponnesian War when Athens was besieged by the Spartans, Aristophanes could still write plays which ridiculed the generals and the whole idea of the War itself. Aristophanes was also very fond of making fun of the serious playwrights, whose plays the audience had seen earlier that same day.

The Greek theatre was very lively, very inventive and they loved mechanical devices. There was a sort of moving trolley which was pushed out with the actors on it to show what was happening inside when the action moved indoors. There was also a kind of crane which could bring the gods on stage, as if they had just arrived from Mount Olympus.

THE THEATRE

Greek theatres were always in the open air and this scene shows a typical performance. Actors were always men and they wore masks to emphasise the characters they were playing. There were normally only two or three actors on stage at a time, but there was also a chorus of 15 or even more who danced, sang and recited to the accompaniment of a pipe. The chorus marked the division between the acts and also drew attention to the important points in the unfolding of the play.

POP-UP SCENE 5
THE THEATRE

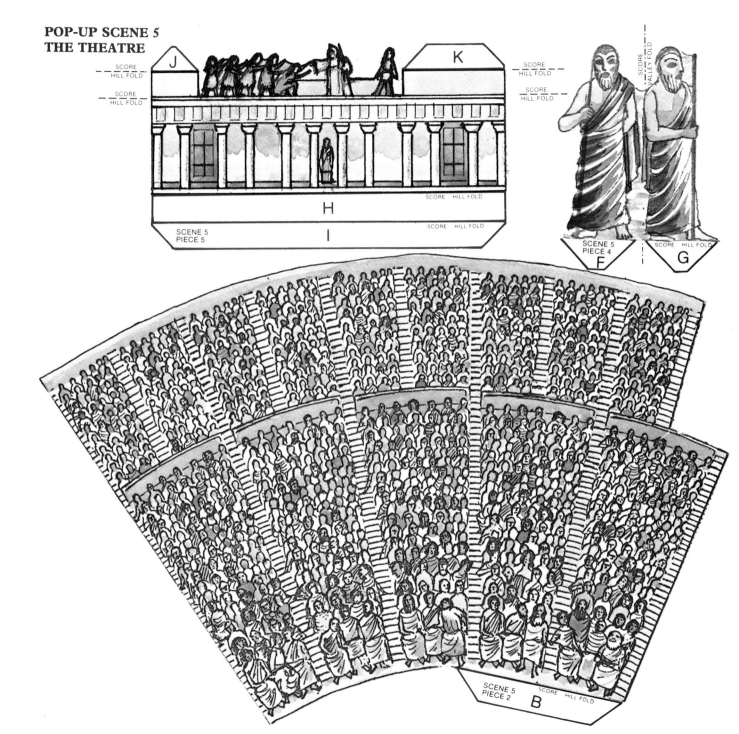

SCORE HILL FOLD

SCORE HILL FOLD

J

K

SCORE HILL FOLD

SCORE HILL FOLD

SCORE VALLEY FOLD

SCORE HILL FOLD

H

I

SCENE 5
PIECE 5

SCENE 5
PIECE 4

F

SCORE HILL FOLD

G

SCENE 5
PIECE 2

SCORE HILL FOLD

B

POP-UP SCENE 6
ALEXANDER THE GREAT AND KING PORUS

SCENE 6 POSITION OF THE PIECES

Although wounded and a prisoner, King Porus stands dignified and serene as he talks to Alexander. This scene shows the end of a battle in which Alexander gained an Indian province for his empire – and a new governor for it, King Porus himself.

SCORE VALLEY FOLD

SCORE HILL FOLD

G

SCENE 6 PIECE 5

H

SCORE HILL FOLD

SCENE 6 PIECE 3

D

SCORE VALLEY FOLD

GLUES BEHIND

F

SCORE HILL FOLD

SCENE 6 PIECE 4

E

SCORE HILL FOLD

ALEXANDER THE GREAT

Although the Greek city states all spoke the same language and shared the same culture, they none the less spent much of their time fighting amongst themselves. As the power of Athens and Sparta weakened, so the power of Macedonia in the North grew. King Philip II of Macedon tried to unify the Greeks under his leadership, but in 336 BC he was murdered and his son Alexander came to the throne. Alexander was 19 and was an amazing young man who made a considerable impression on everyone he came into contact with and indeed his magic has lasted to the present day. Not only was he handsome and brave, but he proved to be one of the greatest generals the world has ever known. He was also imaginative, generous spirited and fired with a love of great poetry and epic deeds. It was said that ever since he was introduced to Homer by his tutor Aristotle that he never slept without one of the books beneath his pillow. He won every battle he fought, but was always merciful to those he defeated and because of his reputation for keeping his word many cities surrendered to him without a fight. With his army he took scholars, poets and administrators to record the wonders they saw and to bring the advantages of Greek civilisation to the peoples they conquered.

After the capture of Tyre he marched South and took Egypt, defeating the Persian king Darius III on the way. At the mouth of the Nile he founded the city of Alexandria which later became one of the greatest centres of learning in the world, eclipsing even Athens as the first city of Greek culture. After visiting the Egyptian temple and monuments and the oracle at Siwa, he set out for the rich lands of the rivers Tigris and Euphrates. After a great victory at Gaugemela, he marched in triumph to Babylon, Suza and Persepolis and was then master of the whole Persian Empire. The prophesy at Gordium had come true.

Darius fled to the east, but was murdered by one of his generals before Alexander could catch up with him. Alexander spent three seasons campaigning in what is now Afghanistan before descending into India and fighting the battle against King Porus which is illustrated in this scene.

There are many stories about so remarkable a man and one of the best known is that of the famous knot of Gordium. It was a large and complicated knot attached to a chariot and it was said that the man who could undo it would be master of Asia. Alexander did not try to untie it, but slashed it with his sword so that it fell apart. People were amazed and impressed by this solution to the puzzle and one reason that the story became so well known was that it exactly reflected his character. Time after time he was able to come up with an unusual and imaginative solution to a difficult problem. One good example was when he wanted to subdue the people of Tyre. The city was built on an island just off the coast and since they were experienced sailors, they were more than a match for Alexander's army on the sea. However he built a causeway across the sea to the island and brought his catapults across it to capture the city. The causeway is still there today.

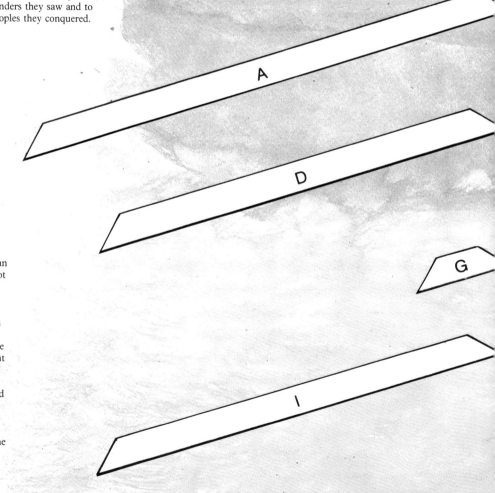

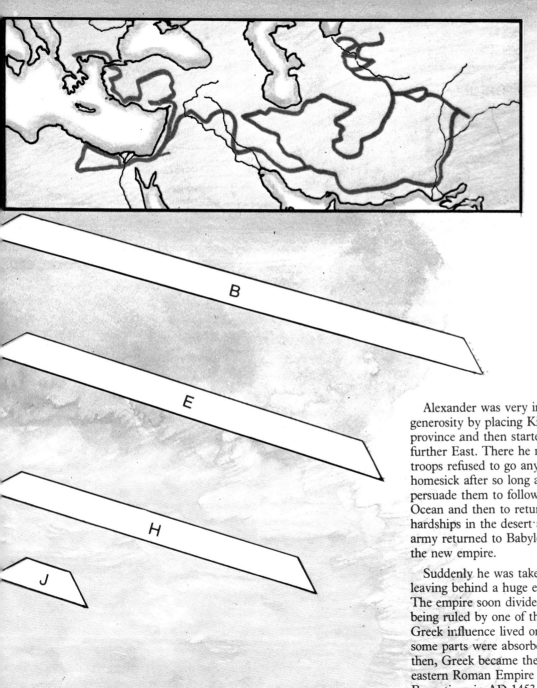

ALEXANDER THE GREAT AND KING PORUS

This scene shows a very important battle that Alexander fought and was one which added an Indian province to his empire. Alexander had first to bring his army across a swollen river and then face a huge enemy army which included 200 elephants, but by brilliant tactics the victory was won. King Porus was wounded and captured. Alexander asked him what he should do with him. "Treat me as a King ought" said Porus. "That is understood" said Alexander, "but is there anything I can do for you personally." "Everything is included in that one request" replied Porus.

Alexander was very impressed. He showed his generosity by placing King Porus in charge of the new province and then started to make plans to go even further East. There he met his first defeat because his troops refused to go any further. They were tired and homesick after so long a time away. He did however persuade them to follow the river down to the Indian Ocean and then to return along the coast. After terrible hardships in the desert and the loss of many men, the army returned to Babylon which was to be the capital of the new empire.

Suddenly he was taken ill and died at the age of 33, leaving behind a huge empire and no proper successor. The empire soon divided into separate kingdoms, each being ruled by one of the generals. Astonishingly, the Greek influence lived on for hundreds of years until some parts were absorbed into the Roman Empire. Even then, Greek became the dominant language of the eastern Roman Empire and it was not until the fall of Byzantium in AD 1453 that Greek influence in Asia finally came to an end.

POP-UP SCENE 6
ALEXANDER THE GREAT AND KING PORUS

SCORE VALLEY FOLD

SCENE 6
PIECE 6

I

SCORE HILL FOLD

SCORE HILL FOLD

J

SCORE VALLEY FOLD

C

GLUES BEHIND

SCENE 6
PIECE 1

A

SCORE HILL FOLD

SCENE 6
PIECE 2

B

SCORE HILL FOLL

MINI COVERS FOR MINI POP-UPS

These five covers are for additional mini pop-ups on certain scenes. First cut the whole page from the book. Then cut out the individual pieces looking at this side.

SCORE VALLEY FOLD

SCORE HILL FOLD

SCORE VALLEY FOLD

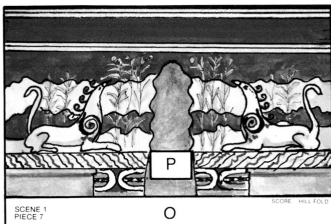

SCENE 1
PIECE 7

P

O

SCORE HILL FOLD

BOTTOM OF FOUR
CARYATIDS
GLUES HERE

M

SCORE HILL FOLD

SCENE 4
PIECE 9

N

SCORE HILL FOLD

THE PARTHENON

This temple, standing proudly on the Acropolis is thought by many people to be the most beautiful in the world. It was built entirely of a white marble and its fluted columns were each slightly tapered and shaped to add to its grace and elegance. Inside was a huge statue of Athene made by the sculptor Pheidias. During the centuries which followed it served first as a Christian church and then as a Moslem mosque. It survived virtually intact until 1687 when a Venetian shell set off some gunpowder stored there by the Turkish garrison. In a second, the masterpiece was badly damaged. Impressive as it is today, we can only imagine how it looked when it was completed in 432 BC.

SCORE HILL FOLD

TOP OF FOUR
CARYATIDS
GLUES HERE

L

SCORE HILL FOLD

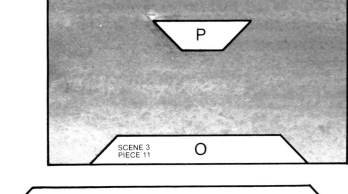

P

SCENE 3
PIECE 11

O

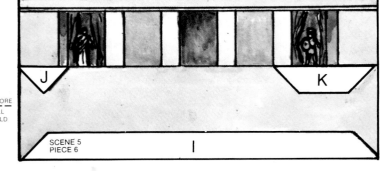

J

K

SCENE 5
PIECE 6

I

MINI COVERS FOR MINI POP-UPS

After removing the whole page from the book cut out the five individual pieces looking at the other side.

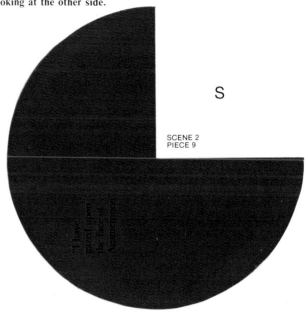

S

SCENE 2
PIECE 9

"I have gazed upon the face of Agamemnon"

HOW TO MAKE THE MINI POP-UPS

Apart from the six main scenes these are six extra mini pop-ups, each of which adds its own contribution to the fascinating story of the Greeks. Five are what are called tableaux and one is an unfolding quadrant.

TO MAKE THE TABLEAUX

Scene 1 The Throne Room at Knossos
Scene 2 The Wooden Horse
Scene 3 Xerxes watches the Battle
Scene 4 The Porch of the Caryatids
Scene 5 Actors at the Theatre

1. Cut out the pieces which make each tableau from the "wings" pages and the mini-covers page.
2. Score and fold as indicated. Crease firmly.
3. Glue the flaps together in alphabetical order.

These sketches show the side views of the tableaux mini pop-ups when upright and when half-closed. Note how the small support is parallel to the base. It will fold completely flat.

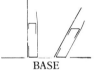

BASE

4. When each tableau is complete it can be glued into position on the base.

TO MAKE THE UNFOLDING QUADRANT

Scene 2 The mask of Agamemnon

1. Cut out the piece keeping well away from the outline.
2. Score along the three diagonals which are marked and crease firmly into hill and valley folds.
3. Cut out precisely.

4. Fold into the quadrant or quarter circle shape as shown in the sketch and glue into position on the base in Scene 2.

AND FINALLY

When all the mini pop-ups are complete and you have finished with these instructions, spread glue on the blue tint on the page and glue it to the blank page opposite. Scene 6 can then be completed.

LEARN SOME ANCIENT GREEK

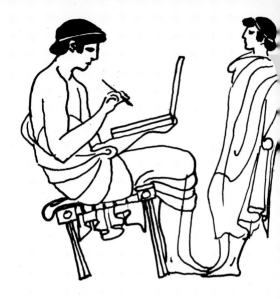

In the ancient world Greek became a language used by far more people than just the Greeks themselves, just as English today is often used by people of many different nationalities to communicate with each other. It was a flexible, subtle language, good for expressing complicated ideas and abstract thought. Like all languages it has gradually changed, but because so many interesting and important books and plays were written in it, people have learnt Ancient Greek as part of their general education through the centuries to the present day.

The Greek alphabet has 24 letters and our word 'alphabet' comes from the first two letters of it. In earliest times Greek was written only in capital letters and with no gaps between the words. Gradually it changed into the script we can recognise today.

Here is the Greek alphabet, showing each capital letter, each small letter, its name and then the nearest English equivalent. To write a Greek word in the English script is called 'transliterating'. If you do that you will often be able to guess what the word is.

Αα	Ββ	Γγ	Δδ	Εε	Ζζ	Ηη	Θθ
alpha	beta	gamma	delta	epsilon	zeta	eta	theta
(a)	(b)	(g)	(d)	(e)	(z)	(e)	(th)
Ιι	Κκ	Λλ	Μμ	Νν	Ξξ	Οο	Ππ
iota	kappa	lambda	mu	nu	xi	omicron	pi
i	(c, k)	(l)	(m)	(n)	(x)	(o)	(p)
Ρρ	Σσς	Ττ	Υυ	Φφ	Χχ	Ψψ	Ωω
rho	sigma	tau	upsilon	phi	chi	psi	omega
(r, rh)	(s)	(t)	(y, u)	(ph)	(ch)	(ps)	(o)

We do not know exactly how the Ancient Greeks pronounced their language, but we can make sensible guesses. It is estimated that about one tenth of modern English words have their origins in Greek. Since many have come to us through Latin, some have changed quite a lot, but others have hardly changed at all.

For instance **ποιητής** transliterates into 'poietes'. In Greek it means 'poet' and the English word is little changed. But **σχολή** is 'schole' and in Greek it meant 'leisure', but it has given us the word 'school'!

Here are some more:

κίνημα (kinema) means in Greek 'movement' and gives us 'cinema' in English.
ἄτομος (atomos) means 'not able to be cut' and gives us the word 'atom'.
φύσις (physis) means 'nature' and gives us 'physics'.